DATE DUE		
MAR 1 7 '95		
MAR 2 9 '95		
APR 1 9 '95		
JUN 2 7 '96		
MAY 08 '98		
DEC 22		
JUL 03 '00		
MAY 1 8 '01		
JUN 28 '01		

Jackson

County

Library

MAR 0 2 1995   **System**

HEADQUARTERS:

413 W. Main

Medford, Oregon 97501

GAYLORD M2G

Cunning
CARNIVORES

Cunning
CARNIVORES

Written by Steve Parker

Scientific Consultant Joyce Pope
Illustrated by Ann Savage,
Chris Orr Illustrations, and Chris Forsey

RSVP
**RAINTREE
STECK-VAUGHN**
P U B L I S H E R S
The Steck-Vaughn Company

Austin, Texas

Library of Congress Cataloging-in-Publication Data
Parker, Steve.
Cunning carnivores/ written by Steve Parker; illustrated by Ann Savage.
p. cm. — (Creepy creatures)
Includes index.
Summary: Describes the physical characteristics and habits of such species of carnivores
as lions, tigers, wolves, dogs, foxes, weasels, bats, and bears.
ISBN 0-8114-2347-6
1. Carnivora—Juvenile literature. [1. Carnivores.]
I. Savage, Ann, 1951- ill. II. Title. III. Series: Parker, Steve. Creepy creatures.
QL737.C2P34   1994
599.74—dc20   93-27256   CIP   AC

Editors: Wendy Madgwick, Susan Wilson
Designer: Janie Louise Hunt

Color reproduction by Global Colour, Malaysia
Printed by L.E.G.O., Vicenza, Italy
1 2 3 4 5 6 7 8 9 0 LE 98 97 96 95 94

Contents

Cunning Carnivores.................................. 6

Big Killer-Cats 8

Lazy Lions 10

Terrific Tigers...................................... 12

Paws, Claws, and Coats............................. 14

Howls and Growls 16

Wily Wolves....................................... 18

Cunning as a Fox................................... 20

Weaselly Weasels 22

Small Carnivores................................... 24

Beware the Bear.................................... 26

Carnivore Cousins 28

Beastly Bats....................................... 30

Killers in the Swim 32

Glossary 34

Index 36

Cunning Carnivores

These are the animals we love to fear. They may seem cute and cuddly, but they can be cunning. They can kill their prey in a hundred different ways. Then they bite and slice the bodies, crunch and munch them into pieces, chew the flesh, crack the bones, and feed until they are full. They are the carnivores — the meat-eaters of the animal world.

◀ The **common raccoon** eats almost anything it can, from birds' eggs and fish to fruit and nuts, and leftover food from trash cans. All 16 members of the raccoon group are carnivores, including coatis and kinkajous.

▶ The **American mink** is in the weasel group. It's a fast and fierce hunter of crabs, crayfish, fish, rats, and birds. All 67 members of the weasel group are carnivores, from otters and sables, to polecats, martens, badgers, and skunks.

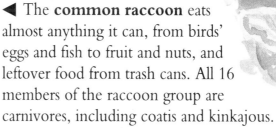

◀ The **Indian brown mongoose** is so quick and agile, that it can dodge a snake's bite and then bite the snake! All 66 members of the mongoose group are carnivores, including civets, linsangs, genets, and meerkats.

▼ People may think of **spotted hyenas** as skulking scavengers. But they are also powerful predators that can capture and kill a full-grown zebra. All four members of the hyena group are carnivores.

▼ The **polar bear** lives in the far north. It hunts seals and fish and eats dying whales and walruses. All seven members of the bear group eat meat, although some also eat leaves and fruits.

▲ The **bobcat** is a stealthy hunter. It lives in rough country, from rocks to swamps, and hunts small animals such as rabbits and mice. All 35 members of the cat group are carnivores, from huge lions and tigers to small but fierce wildcats and pet cats.

◄ The **golden jackal** from Africa and southern Asia is a member of the dog family. It hunts all types of creatures, from gazelles to frogs. All 35 members of the dog group are carnivores, from timber wolves and coyotes to foxes and pet dogs.

Big Killer-Cats

The big cats are the supreme hunters of the carnivore world. Their killing tools are long teeth and sharp claws, on a powerful, agile body. There are seven kinds of big cats. They include the lion and tiger and the five shown here.

▼ The **snow leopard** is rare and beautiful. Its home is the high mountains of the Middle East and Central Asia, where it feeds on large deer, wild sheep, boars, hares, rabbits, and birds. It is also known as the **ounce**.

◄ The **cheetah** from Africa and the Middle East is famous as the world's fastest land animal. It has a slim, supple body, very long legs, and a surprisingly small head. Cheetahs can sprint at 60 miles (100km) per hour. They feed on medium-sized gazelles and impalas, as well as hares and game birds.

▶ The **jaguar** is South America's only big cat. It also dwells in Central America and Mexico. Jaguars are similar to leopards in many ways. They hunt all types of prey, from deer and wild pigs to caimans and turtles, rats and mice, fish and birds.

◀ The most adaptable of the big cats, the **leopard** lives throughout Africa and southern Asia. It can survive in many habitats, from mountains to tropical forests, dry grassland, and almost into city suburbs. When it rests up in the trees, the leopard is almost perfectly camouflaged in the leafy shadows.

▶ More than any other big cat, the **clouded leopard** is at home in the trees. It catches birds and small animals there, or it drops silently from a branch onto an unwary deer or wild pig passing below. The clouded leopard is about 3 feet (1m) long with a tail almost as long as its body. It is found in Southeast Asia.

Lazy Lions

Lions are the only cats that live in groups. The group is called a pride. It may seem a lazy life, as the adult lions doze in the hot African sun, and the cubs pounce and play with each other. Lions can be dangerous, too. Female lions must kill to eat, and they risk the kicking hooves and jabbing horns of their prey. Male lions must defend the pride against all comers. If food is scarce, the cubs may starve.

▼ You can instantly identify a male **lion** by his shaggy mane. He wanders around the edge of his pride's area, roaring fiercely. He also sprays urine on rocks and plants to mark the boundary. The chief male defends his pride against strange males and against other animals who pose a danger. Sometimes a male lion from another area tries to take over. The two may fight to the death.

▶ The **lionesses** do most of the hunting. They stealthily stalk their prey, such as a zebra, wildebeest, or gazelle. Their tawny coats camouflage the lionesses in the dry grass and bush.

◀ The hunting lions charge from cover and fasten their teeth and claws onto the victim. They try to avoid serious injury from the hooves and horns of their prey.

▶ Soon the prey is dead. The male **lions** eat first, then the females, and the cubs last. When times are hard, and food is short, there may be nothing left for the cubs.

▶ Newborn **lion cubs** feed on their mother's milk. A lioness may give milk to cubs of other females in the pride. Usually, all the pride females are related. They are mothers, daughters, sisters, grand-daughters, aunts, and nieces.

Terrific Tigers

In the dense woodland of an Indian mountainside in the fading light of dusk, there is a deep, fearsome roar. It is a tiger telling the whole countryside that this area is occupied — other tigers keep away! Soon this biggest of the big cats will be creeping quietly towards a deer, its meal for the next few days.

▼ **Tigers** once lived in the Middle East, across India and Southeast Asia, all the way to the islands of Java and Bali. Then they were killed in such huge numbers that they disappeared from most of these areas. They now survive mainly in special nature preserves. Tigers are still very rare, and they are protected by wildlife laws.

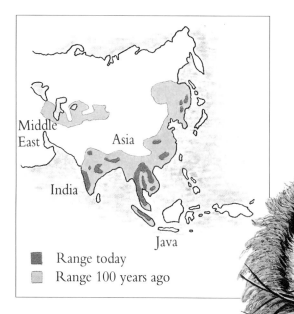

Middle
East   Asia

India

Java

■ Range today
■ Range 100 years ago

▶ When it has crept to within 60 feet (18m) of prey, the tiger rushes out. In a few bounds, it knocks its prey to the ground. Then the tiger grabs the animal's throat and suffocates it.

► Unlike the lion, the **tiger** lives alone. A big male tiger is 10 feet (3m) long, 3 feet high (1m) at the shoulder, and weighs over 550 pounds (250kg) — more massive than 10 eight-year-old children.

◄ The **tiger** hunts by silent stealth. Its stripes hide it among the shadows and stems of thick undergrowth. Hunting takes a long time. Of the animals it tracks, the tiger catches only about one in ten.

▲ A hungry **tiger** may eat over 50 pounds (23kg) of food at one meal. That's the same as 200 quarter-pound hamburgers! Only skin and bones are left.

► **Tigers** like water. They drink a lot, especially when eating. They swim well, and they lie or stand in a swampy pool to keep cool.

Paws, Claws, and Coats

There are about 28 kinds of small and medium-size cats around the world. They may not be as fearsome as huge lions and tigers, but to their prey, they are just as deadly! These cats were once hunted for their fur. Sadly, many are now very rare. Hunting them is generally banned by international wildlife laws.

▶ The **mountain lion** has almost as many names as it has coat colors. It is also called the **cougar**, **puma**, and **panther**. This cunning cat lives in many habitats, from southern Canada down to the tip of South America.

▶ The **golden cat** spends its life in the forests of Africa. It is so stealthy and secretive that little is known about its habits. It sleeps in trees by day, and hunts in trees by night.

▼ The **lynx** is a well-known cat from North America, Europe, and Asia. It has a very short tail and tufted cheeks and ears. Like most cats, it is nocturnal (active at night). In North America its favorite food is snowshoe hare.

▲ Like a smaller version of the cheetah, the **serval** is a swift predator found in African grasslands. It pursues small deer, rabbits, and hares. And it can spring up to 10 feet (3m) high to catch a bird in midair.

◄ Rarely seen, **Pallas's cat** is thickset and strong, with a head and body about 2 feet (60cm) long. It is a secretive hunter of rats, mice, hares, and birds, in the grasslands and rocky hills of central and eastern Asia.

▼ This may look like a pet cat, but beware. It is the pet cat's distant ancestor — the **wildcat**. Wildcats live in North America, northern Britain, Europe, Africa, and Asia. People have tried to tame wildcats, but they can turn wild at any time.

Howls and Growls

Cats are built for stealth, and most live alone. Dogs are tireless runners, and most live in groups. They have long, strong legs, and they can track their prey for many hours at a "dog-trot." The dog group includes the wild dogs shown here, wolves, and foxes.

▶ **Asian wild dogs** are also known as **dholes**. Several family groups band together as a pack, and they can bring down victims as big as water buffaloes. A hungry dhole can eat 10 pounds (4.5kg) of meat in less than an hour.

▲ **African hunting dogs** are expert group predators. There may be over 50 in a pack, working together and taking turns in the hunt. They choose a victim, such as a zebra or wildebeest, and pursue it "doggedly" until it is "dog-tired." Then they bite and snap at its feet, hold its nose and tail, pull it to the ground, and rip out its insides.

▲ The **dingo** came to Australia many thousands of years ago, probably as a semi-tame companion of the aboriginal people. Since then, dingos have roamed wild in the outback. They live in family groups and eat kangaroos, wallabies, and farm animals.

▲ The **bush dog** of Central and South America is probably the best swimmer in the dog group. It preys on various small animals, and may dive underwater after them. Bush dogs live in small packs and prefer forests and swamps.

◀▲ The **coyote** — farmer's friend or foe? Coyotes attack farm animals — from cattle to chickens. But they also eat rabbits, rats, and similar animals. These wild dogs have spread across North and Central America.

People once thought that **coyotes** were solitary animals. Now we know that they sometimes live in packs, like wolves. They howl to tell other coyotes to keep away and to keep in touch with their pack.

Wily Wolves

The eerie howl of the wolf strikes fear into all kinds of animals, from huge moose to small rabbits. The gray wolf is the biggest member of the dog group. Even in ancient times, it was known as a killer of farm animals and, occasionally, people. In those long-ago times, people bred some wolves to be friendly. Over thousands of years they produced the pet dogs we have today.

▲ **Gray wolves** live in groups called packs. There are usually from five to ten wolves in a pack. The pack is made up of a chief male and female, their babies, and other youngsters.

▶ You can see the **wolf's** dog-like features, particularly its long, spear-shaped teeth. They are known as canine teeth. All carnivores have them — they are used for ripping and tearing meat.

▶ **Wolves** hunt together, and they can bring down large deer such as moose or caribou. They also eat smaller animals, including beavers, hares, and fish.

▼ A **wolf** howls when it is separated from the pack or to warn neighboring packs to keep away. The howls carry over 5 miles (8km) through the still night air.

▲ **Wolves** "talk" to each other by grunts, whines, barks, and yips, and also by body language. Body language is the position of their face, ears, body, and tail. A senior, or dominant, wolf snarls and holds its tail high. A junior wolf cowers, puts its ears back, and lowers its tail.

▼ The **maned wolf** dwells in the prairies and scrub forest of central South America. It is not a true wolf, but more a relation of the foxes. The maned wolf is big, and has a wolflike face. This rare creature eats birds, rats, rabbits, fish, lizards, and anything else it can catch – including armadillos!

▲ The **red wolf** of southeastern North America is so rare that there are hardly any left in the wild.

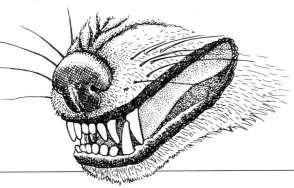

Cunning as a Fox

There are many tales about foxes, from ancient times to today. The stories are endless, and most show the fox's clever cunning. Indeed, this cunning has made the red fox the most abundant of all carnivores. Here, it is joined by a few of the 20 other kinds of foxes.

▲ The **Indian fox** is probably the most typical member of the foxes. It has large triangular ears, a long snout, thick fur, and a bushy tail known as a brush.

◀ Also called the **common zorro**, the **crab-eating fox** comes from South America. It eats much more than crabs! Like most foxes, it gulps down whatever it can find, from mice and rats to birds, lizards, snakes, frogs, crabs, fishes, insects, fruits, berries, eggs … and anything else it can find.

▼ Alert and aware, the **red fox** has excellent eyesight, hearing, and smell. It usually hunts at night and eats rats, mice, rabbits, birds, insects, fruits, and berries. It may also raid hen houses and steal edible leftovers from garbage.

▲ The **arctic fox** makes its living in one of the harshest places on Earth — the snowy lands of the far north. In the fall, its gray-brown summer coat is replaced by thick, white winter fur. This gives great camouflage for creeping up on birds, hares, and lemmings.

▶ **Swift foxes** dwell in prairies and rocky scrublands, from Mexico, north through the Midwest states, to Canada. Some fox experts say that the kit fox, with its bigger ears and smaller body, is a type of swift fox.

▶ The **fennec fox** is the smallest member of the dog group, with a head and body just 15 inches (38cm) long. Its huge ears listen for mice, insects, lizards, and birds, in the deserts of North Africa and the Middle East. The ears also give off heat, so the fox does not get too hot.

Weaselly Weasels

The weasel group of carnivores is made up mostly of small, long, slim creatures, ideally shaped for pursuing mice, rats, and rabbits into their burrows. They are fast-moving hunters of all kinds of animals. Badgers and skunks are also in the weasel family of carnivores.

▼ The **striped skunk** must hold the record as worst-smelling carnivore! It warns attackers by stamping its front feet, raising its tail, and walking stiff-legged. If this display is ignored it does a handstand and sprays terrible-smelling fluid from under its tail.

▲ The **black-footed ferret** of the prairies, one of the rarest carnivores, eats prairie dogs.

▼ The smallest carnivore, with a head and body only 8 inches (20cm) long, the **least weasel** can follow a mouse into its burrow.

▶ The **wolverine** has a fearsome reputation, and it is very strong for its size. This small bearlike creature has been known to kill large deer, such as caribou.

▶ The **American badger** eats many kinds of foods, from worms to chipmunks, birds, and reptiles — and their eggs. This powerful digger usually hides by day in its burrow.

◀ The **American marten**, a typical member of the weasel family, is quick and agile. It has a good sense of smell and hearing, sharp eyes — and sharp teeth! It lives in trees and catches squirrels.

▶ **Sables** live in the cold regions of northern Asia and in Japan. People hunted and killed sables, using their fur to make fur coats. Now, sables are raised on fur farms, so fewer are caught in the wild.

▶ Otters are excellent swimmers, at home in the water and out of it. **Sea otters** of the Pacific coasts live almost all their lives in the sea. They eat shellfish such as mussels and abalones, hitting them with a rock to crack their shells.

Small Carnivores

These animals are from two main groups of carnivores. The first, the raccoons, include the coatis, kinkajous, and olingos. They come from North and South America. The other, the large mongoose group, includes the catlike civets, linsangs, and genets. These come from Europe and Asia.

▶ More like a cat than a mongoose, the **banded linsang** is an expert climber. It roams the forests of central Africa, catching birds and insects.

▼ **Coatis** roam in groups of about 20 to 40 in the forests of South America. They probe with their flexible noses, sniffing out worms, insects, spiders, and other small snacks.

▶ The mongoose is a busy, active animal, searching out all kinds of prey such as rats and mice, spiders and scorpions, and snakes and lizards. The **banded mongoose** lives in Africa. It often steals eggs, and breaks them open by throwing them against a stone. It then licks up the contents.

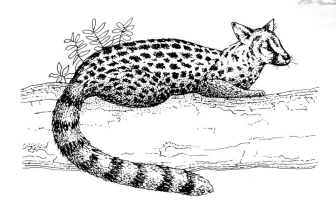

◀ The **common genet** is an animal whose range is widespread. This stealthy catlike hunter is found in southern Europe, Africa, and the Middle East. In ancient times, people in Mediterranean lands kept genets as pets to kill rats, mice, and other pests.

▶ More like a dog than a mongoose, the **African civet** is a strong hunter of birds, reptiles, frogs, and insects.

◀ Most Americans know the **raccoon**. It is thought of as a cute pet or as annoying pest, raiding eggs from the henhouse and scavenging from the city dump. Raccoons survive almost everywhere and eat almost anything.

Beware the Bear

Teddy bears are cute cuddly toys and real baby bears look cute and cuddly, too. But full-grown bears are incredibly strong, and they can change mood without warning. One moment, they may be peacefully munching fruit. The next moment, they may charge at you with terrible ferocity. Always beware of the bear.

▲ The **American black bear** looks like a smaller version of the grizzly bear. Black bears sleep for most of the winter. The cubs, which are usually born in January, remain in the den with the female until late spring.

◀ This animal is called a **panda bear**, but it's not a true bear. You probably know it as the **giant panda**. It is very rare, lives in highland China, and eats almost nothing but bamboo shoots. The panda has many body similarities with bears. So it is included in the same group, as the only "carnivore" that rarely eats meat!

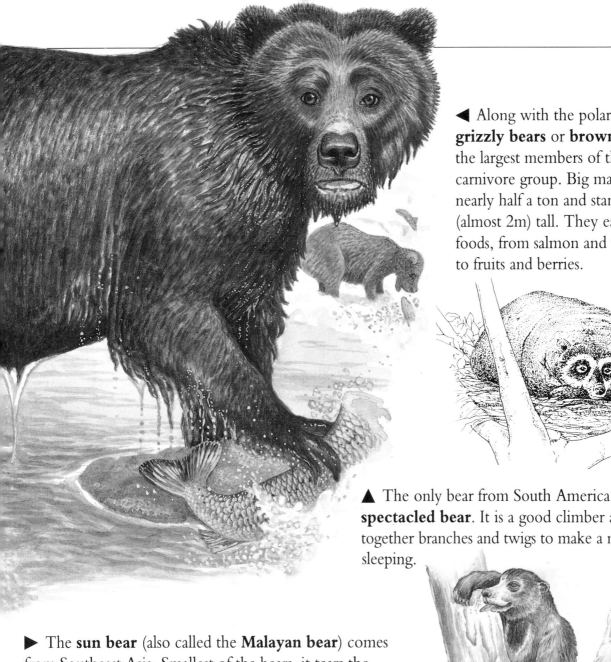

◄ Along with the polar bears, the **grizzly bears** or **brown bears** are the largest members of the whole carnivore group. Big males weigh nearly half a ton and stand 8 feet (almost 2m) tall. They eat many foods, from salmon and young deer, to fruits and berries.

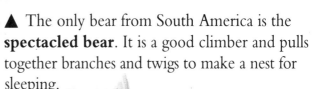

▲ The only bear from South America is the **spectacled bear**. It is a good climber and pulls together branches and twigs to make a nest for sleeping.

► The **sun bear** (also called the **Malayan bear**) comes from Southeast Asia. Smallest of the bears, it tears the bark off trees with its long claws, and gobbles up the grubs, termites, and other creepy-crawlies beneath.

◄ The **Asian black bear** eats mainly nuts, fruits, and young leaves. It will also smash open a bees' nest and eat the honey. So how can it be a carnivore? Because it belongs to the bear family, which is part of the carnivore group. It just happens that this bear has a mainly herbivorous (plant-eating) way of life.

Carnivore Cousins

All of the animals you have seen so far in this book belong to the group of mammals called Carnivora. Of the 4,000 kinds of mammals, about 230 belong to the Carnivora group. Yet many other mammals also eat meat. Here are some of them. They are just as fierce, cunning, and deadly as their Carnivora cousins.

◀ Very few mammals have a venomous bite. The **Cuban solenodon** is one. This rare forest creature from the Caribbean island of Cuba poisons and feasts on insects, lizards, mice, and small birds.

▲ The **brown bandicoot** is a rat-like creature from eastern and southern Australia. This animal is a marsupial, or pouched mammal. It eats all kinds of worms, insects, and grubs. It also hunts scorpions, but first nips the stingers from their tails.

▶ In Australian forests, the **quoll** or **Eastern native-cat** prowls through the night looking for small animals to eat. Quolls are not true cats. They are marsupials – pouched mammals related to kangaroos and koalas.

◀ **Tree shrews** are small, quick creatures from Southeast Asia. They eat a variety of small animals, from lizards to beetles, and can snatch a moth or small bird in midair.

▼ The **shrew** may be small, but it squeaks and shrieks loudly if it is threatened. Shrews must eat their own weight in food each day, or they die of hunger. A fat, juicy worm is a magnificent banquet!

▲ Fewer beasts are fiercer than the **Tasmanian devil**, which lives on the island of Tasmania, part of Australia. Its strong jaws and teeth can easily crunch through skin and bones.

Beastly Bats

Some of the creepiest, most cunning carnivores fly under cover of night and swoop out of the darkness onto their prey. They are bats. There are almost 1,000 kinds of bats around the world. A few feed on fruits and plants, but most are aerial hunter-killers. They prey on other animals from those as small as a mosquito, to others as huge as a horse!

▲ Few bats are at home on the ground, but the **American false vampire** is. It creeps on all fours towards a mouse or small bird, leaps onto the victim, and breaks its head or neck with a quick crack.

◀ The **white bat** from Central and South America is a truly ghostly creature. Its fur is very pale, and it looks like a winged ghost as it chases moths and other insects.

▼ A favorite snack for the **slit-faced bat** is a scorpion, which it catches by swooping down to the ground. It also hunts poisonous spiders and centipedes.

▲ Several kinds of bats skim low over water, catching fish and other water-dwellers with their long, sharp claws. This is the **fish-eating bat** of western Mexico.

▲ Almost all hunting bats fly at night, and the **noctule** is no exception. It is quite large for a bat, measuring 14 inches (34cm) from one wingtip to the other. It crunches up crickets, big beetles, and bugs.

▶ The big **brown bat** of North America feasts on all kinds of insects. Like most bats, it gives out very high-pitched squeaks, and listens for the returning echoes. The pattern of echoes tell the bat the positions of things surrounding it, even in pitch blackness.

Killers in the Swim

Cunning meat-eaters are found not only on the land and in the air. They hunt in the world's waters, too. From water shrews in a local pool to killer whales in the ocean deep, carnivorous killers go anywhere that there is flesh to eat.

▶ Not for nothing is this huge beast called the **killer whale**. A large male is 30 feet (about 9m) and 4 tons of speed-swimming, death-dealing cunning. Killer whales are also known as **orcas**. They hunt seabirds, seals and sea lions, fish, and even their whale cousins.

▲ The **desman** is a member of the mole group. It is a rare creature from eastern Europe and central Asia. The desman lives in brooks and pools in remote areas, and feeds on fish, frogs, crayfish, and other water life.

▼ **Water shrews** do not have to live near water. They survive fairly well in dry grassland. But they are good swimmers and pursue tadpoles, water insects, fish, and frogs.

◄ The **leopard seal** is a sea-dwelling hunter. It has rows of sharp teeth and can move with amazing bursts of speed and agility. It is a fearless hunter of penguins, fish, and other seals.

▶ The **bottle-nosed dolphin** is cute and clever – but it is still a killer. Groups of dolphins surround and devour fish, squid, and other sea animals.

Glossary

Adaptable In the animal world, a creature that can live in a variety of different habitats, or places, is adaptable. Places include swamps and mountains, forests and scrublands.

Body language Positions of the head, body, and limbs that give out information and messages. For example, a wolf that shows its teeth is aggressive and may attack.

Brush A name for a long, bushy tail, especially the fox's tail.

Camouflage Colors, shapes, and patterns that blend in with the surroundings and hide an animal from predators.

Canine A type of tooth that is long and pointed, like a spear, for jabbing into prey and ripping flesh. Most carnivorous mammals have four big canine teeth. Also another name for dog.

Carnivora The scientific name for a group of mammals that is mostly made up of meat-eaters, or carnivores. There are seven main subgroups in the Carnivora group. These are the cats (felids), dogs (canids), weasels (mustelids), bears (ursids), mongooses (viverrids), raccoons (procyonids), and hyenas (hyenids).

Carnivore A creature that eats meat, or other animals.

Carnivorous Feeding on meat or animals.

Dominant In nature, an animal that has a high position or rank in its group — the "chief" or "boss." Dominant animals usually get the best food, shelter, and mates compared to the more junior or submissive members.

Echo A sound that has bounced back from an object. Bats use the echoes of their high-pitched squeaks to locate objects and find their way in the dark. This is called echolocation.

Eggs Small rounded objects that are laid by a female animal and that can hatch and grow into youngsters. Birds, reptiles, and many insects lay eggs.

Grub A common name for the small, worm-shaped maggot, or other insect larva.

Habitat The place in which an organism lives. Habitats include desert, evergreen forest, rain forest, rocky seashore, grassland, deep sea, or sandy seashore. Most plants and animals are adapted to living in one, or a few similar, habitats.

Herbivorous Eating plants and plant parts, such as leaves, stems, flowers, roots, wood, or seeds.

Mammal An animal with a backbone, warm blood, and a body covering of fur or hair, that feeds its babies on milk.

Marsupial A mammal whose young complete their development in the female's pocket or pouch. Marsupial mammals include kangaroos, koalas, wombats, and bandicoots.

Nocturnal Active at night.

Outback The local name for the dry scrubland, bushland, and semi-desert toward the middle of Australia.

Pack The name for a group of certain types of animals, usually hunting animals, such as dogs or wolves.

Predator An animal that hunts other animals for food. Carnivores are predators.

Prey An animal that is hunted for food by other animals.

Pride The name for a group of lions.

Scavenger An animal that feeds on leftovers from other animals' meals, pieces of dead animals and plants, and similar scraps.

Suffocate To prevent an animal from breathing, so that it dies from lack of air. Some carnivores clamp their jaws onto the neck of their prey, closing the windpipe that carries air down to the lungs. This causes suffocation by strangling.

Venomous Poisonous.

Index

A
African civet 25
African hunting dog 16
American badger 23
American black bear 26
American false vampire bat 30
American marten 23
American mink 6
arctic fox 21
Asian black bear 27
Asian wild dog (dhole) 16

B
banded linsang 24
banded mongoose 25
bats 30–31
    feeding in 30, 31
bears 26–27
    feeding in 26, 27
black-footed ferret 22
bobcat 7
bottle-nosed dolphin 33
brown bandicoot 28
brown bat 31
brown bear 27
bush dog 17

C
camouflage 21
canine teeth 18
Carnivora 28
cats 7, 8–15
    feeding in 8, 9, 11, 13
cheetah 8
clouded leopard 9
coatis 24
common genet 25
common raccoon 6
common zorro (crab-eating fox) 20
cougar 14
coyote 17
crab-eating fox 20
Cuban solenodon 28

D
desman 33
dhole 16
dingo 17
dogs 7, 16–17
    hunting in 16, 17, 19, 25

E
Eastern native-cat 29

F
fennec fox 21
fish-eating bat 31
foxes 20–21

G
golden cat 14
golden jackal 7
gray wolf 18
grizzly bear (brown bear) 27

I
Indian brown mongoose 6
Indian fox 20

J
jaguar 9

K
killer whale (orca) 32
kit fox 21

L
least weasel 22
leopard 9
leopard seal 33
lions 8, 10–11
    cubs 11
    hunting 11
    lionesses 11
lynx 15

M
Malayan bear 27
maned wolf 19
marsupials 29
mongoose 6
mountain lion (cougar, puma, panther) 14

N
noctule 31

O
orca 32
ounce 8

P

Pallas's cat 15
panda bear (giant panda) 26
panther 14
polar bear 7
puma 14

Q

quoll (Eastern native-cat) 29

R

raccoons 6, 24, 25
red fox 21
red wolf 19

S

sables 23
sea otter 23

serval 15
shrew 29
slit-faced bat 31
snow leopard (ounce) 8
spectacled bear 27
spotted hyena 7
striped skunk 22
    display in 22
sun bear (Malayan bear) 27
swift fox 21

T

Tasmanian devil 29
tigers 8, 12–13
    behavior 13
    hunting in 12, 13
    range 12
tree shrews 29

W

water shrew 33
weasels 6, 22–23
white bat 30
wildcat 15
wolverine 22
wolves 18–19
    behavior 19
    hunting in 18, 19
    packs of 18, 19

A TEMPLAR BOOK

Devised and produced by The Templar Company plc
Pippbrook Mill, London Road, Dorking,
Surrey RH4 1JE, Great Britain

PHOTOGRAPHIC CREDITS

t = top, b = bottom, l = left, r = right
All photographs are from Frank Lane Picture Agency (FLPA)
page 8 F. Pölking/FLPA; *page 9* Silvestris/FLPA; *page 11* E.C.D. Hosking/
FLPA; *page 13t* Silvestris/FLPA; *page 13b* Silvestris/FLPA; *page 15t*
A. Hamblin/FLPA; *page 15b* R. Bender/FLPA; *page 16* P. Perry/FLPA;
page 19t W. Wisniewski/FLPA; *page 19b* Silvestris/FLPA;
page 21t L. Lee Rue/FLPA; *page 21b* M. van Nostrand/FLPA;
page 23t W.L. Miller/FLPA; *page 23b* E. & D. Hosking/FLPA;
page 24 Silvestris/FLPA; *page 26* T. Whittaker/FLPA;
page 29 E. & D. Hosking/FLPA